Jazz Styles

Level One

Supplement to All Piano and Keyboard Methods

Original Music by John Revezoulis

Foreword

Jazz styles, evolving over many years, encompass a broad range including ragtime, blues, boogie, swing and rock. A casual, improvisational attitude is the common thread. The syncopated rhythms and harmonies have remained popular for many generations and provide fascinating educational material.

Pieces with 4/4 and common time signatures are conceived as cut time. Therefore, the tempo indications should be interpreted with cut time in mind. The cut time signature has not been used because of the limitations of Level One. Explanation of cut time may be done at the discretion of the teacher.

Index

SCHAUM PUBLICATIONS, INC.
10235 N. Port Washington Rd. • Mequon, WI 53092

www.schaumpiano.net

ISBN 13: 978-1-62906-012-5

0331

Let's Boogie

John Revezoulis

Pieces with 4/4 and common time signatures are conceived as cut time. Therefore, the tempo indications should be interpreted with cut time in mind. The cut time signature has not been used because of the limitations of Level One. Explanation of cut time may be done at the discretion of the teacher.

1
p

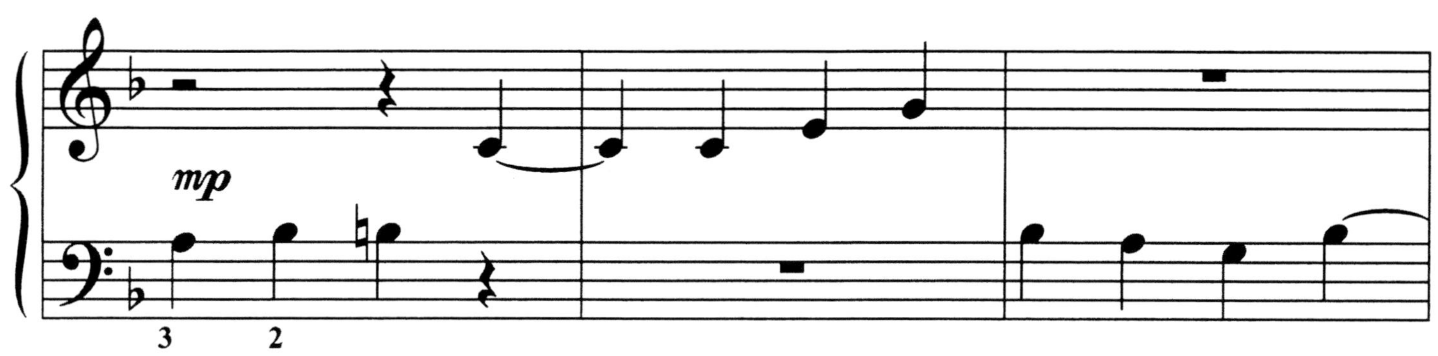
mp
3 2

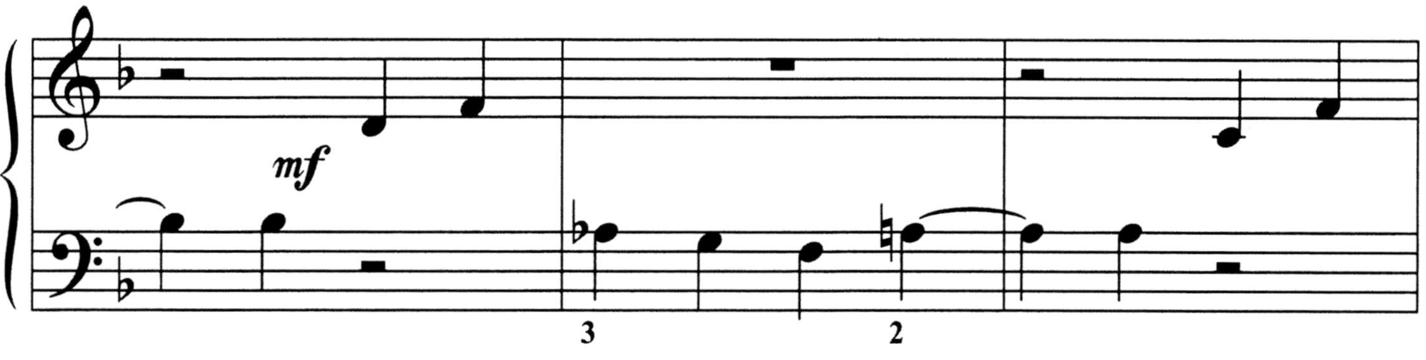
mf
3 2

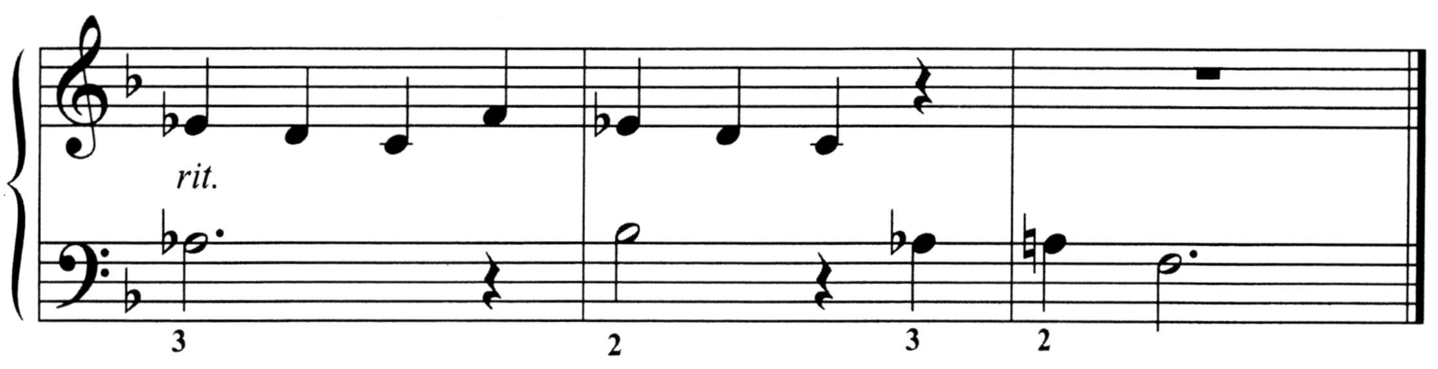
rit.
3 2 3 2

Calypso Rag

Spiritoso

John Revezoulis

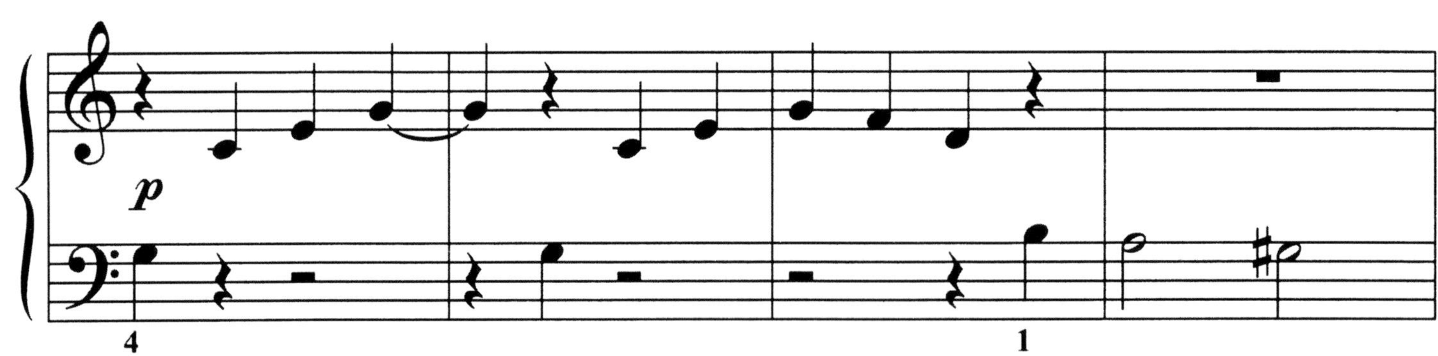

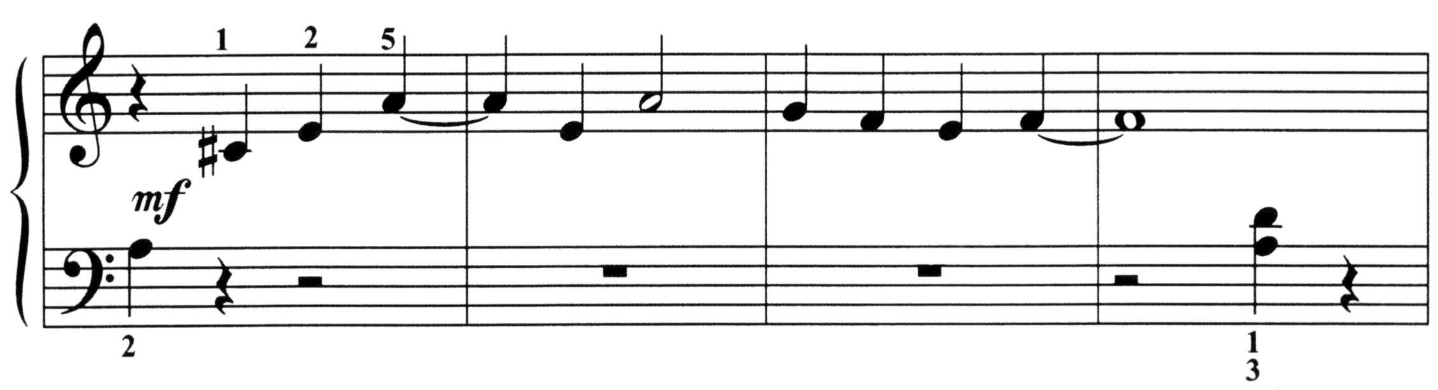

1
mf
4
1

p

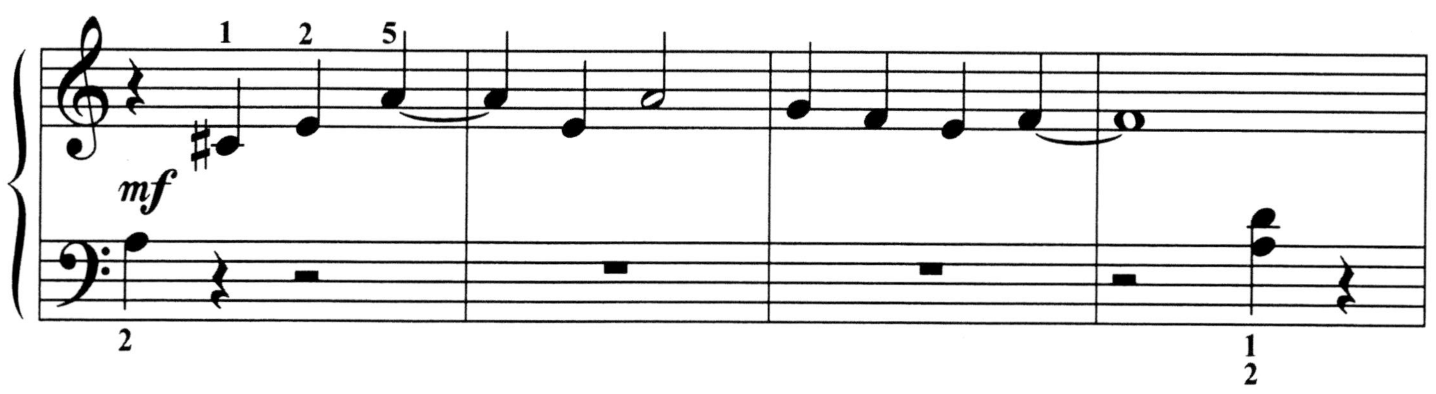
1
2
5
mf
2
1
2

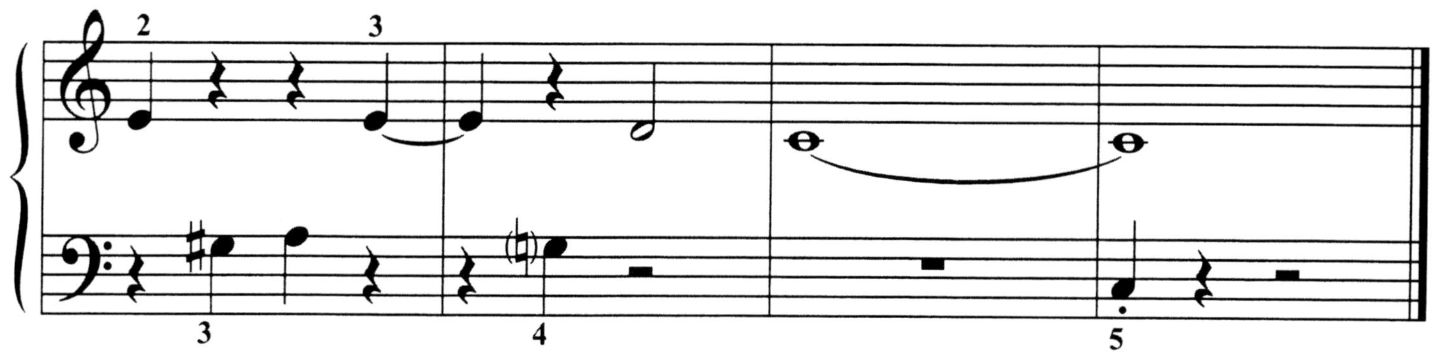
2
3
3
4
5

Rock Boogie

Energico

John Revezoulis

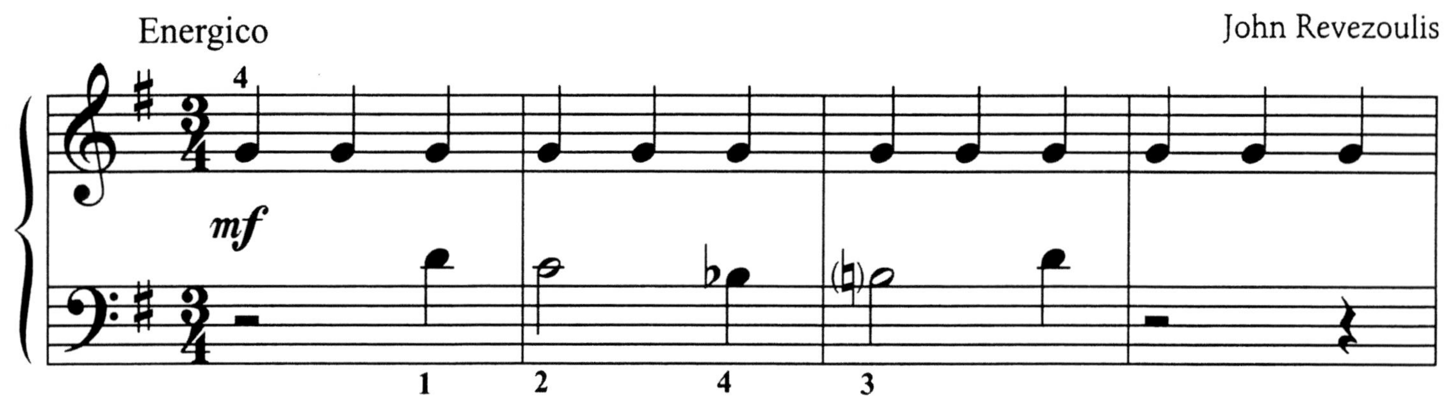

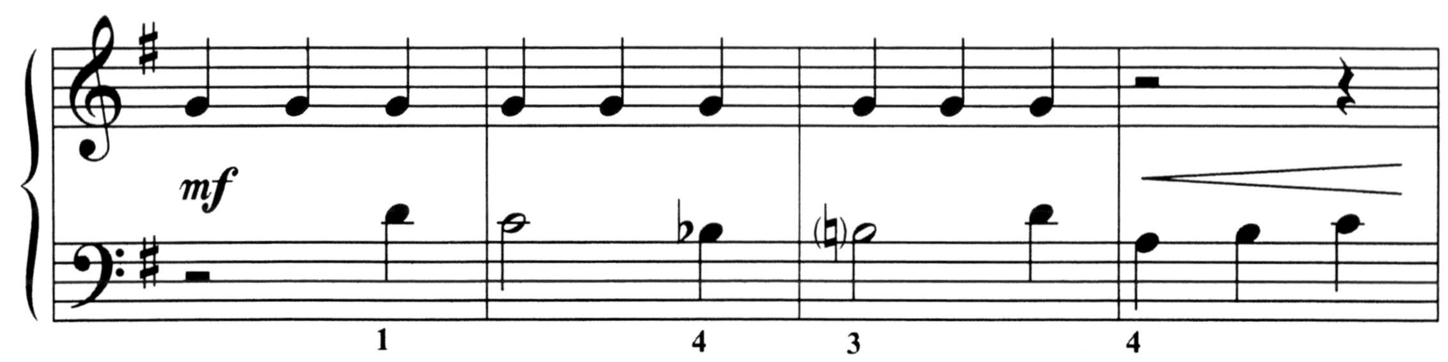

f
mf
mp
poco a poco
accelerando
f

From Rag to Blues

Allegretto

John Revezoulis

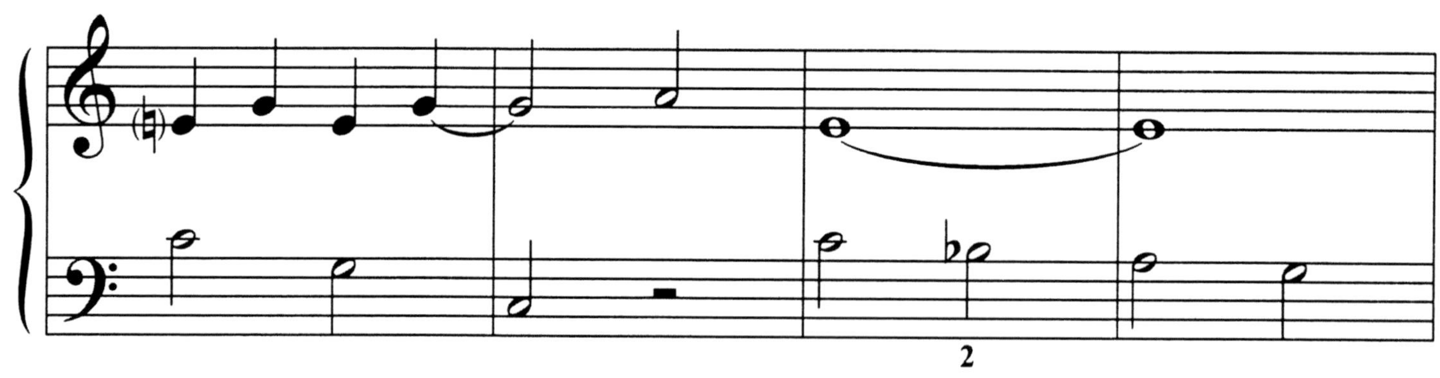

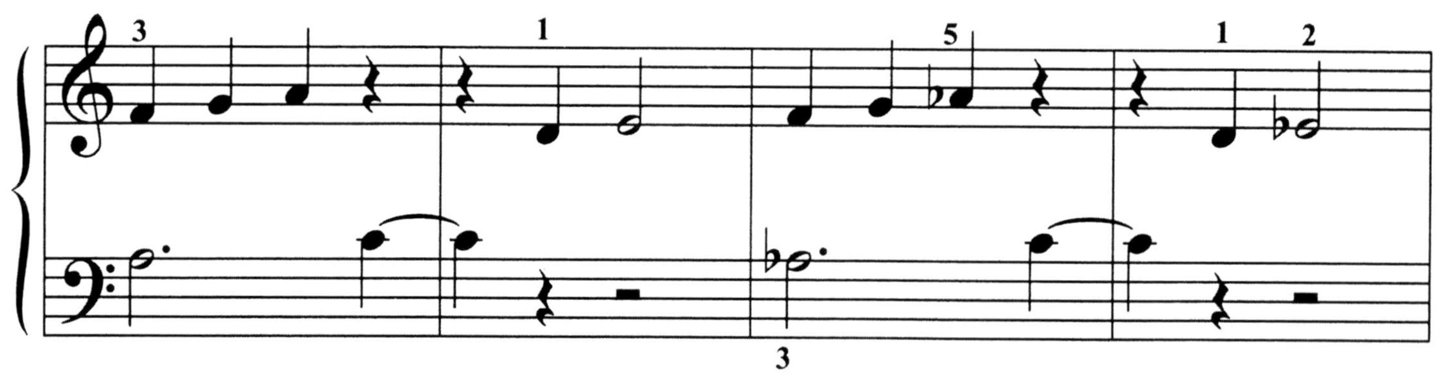

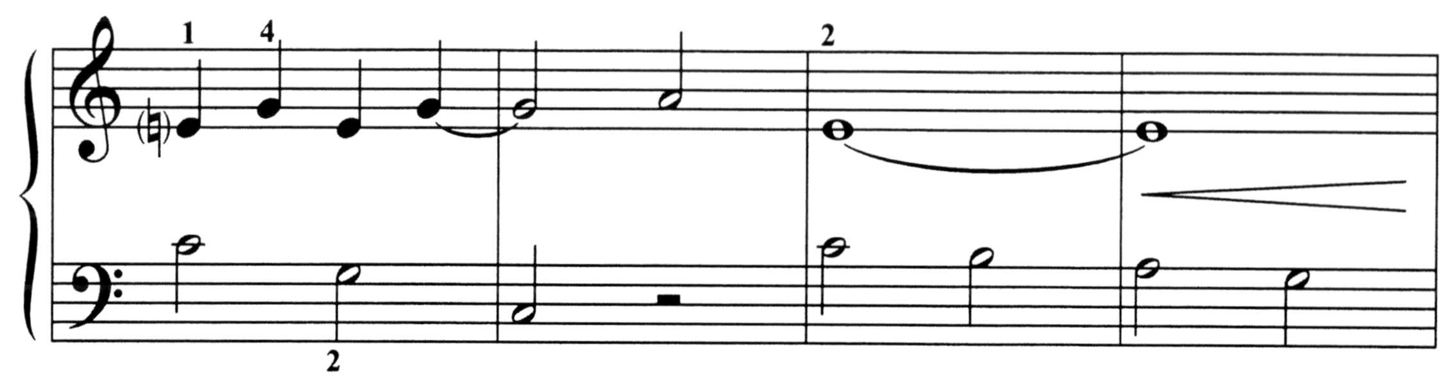

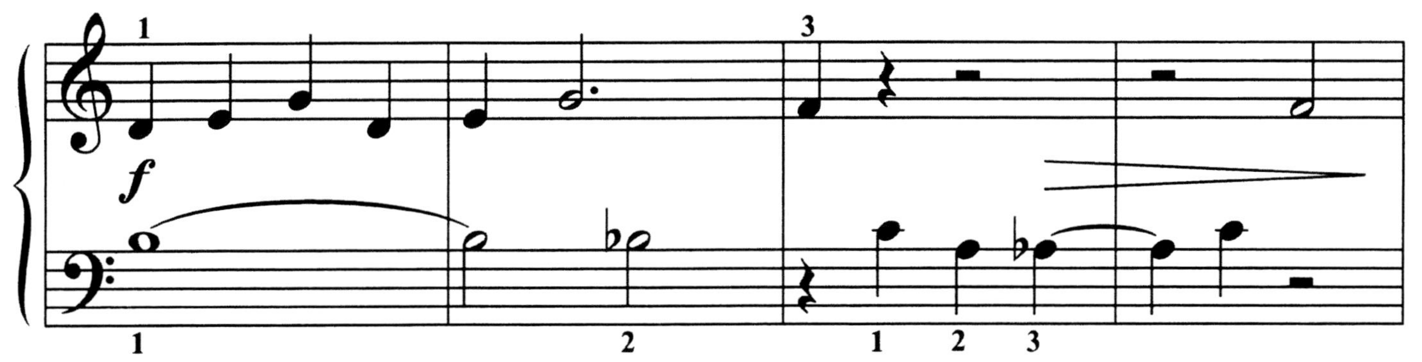
f

mf

mp

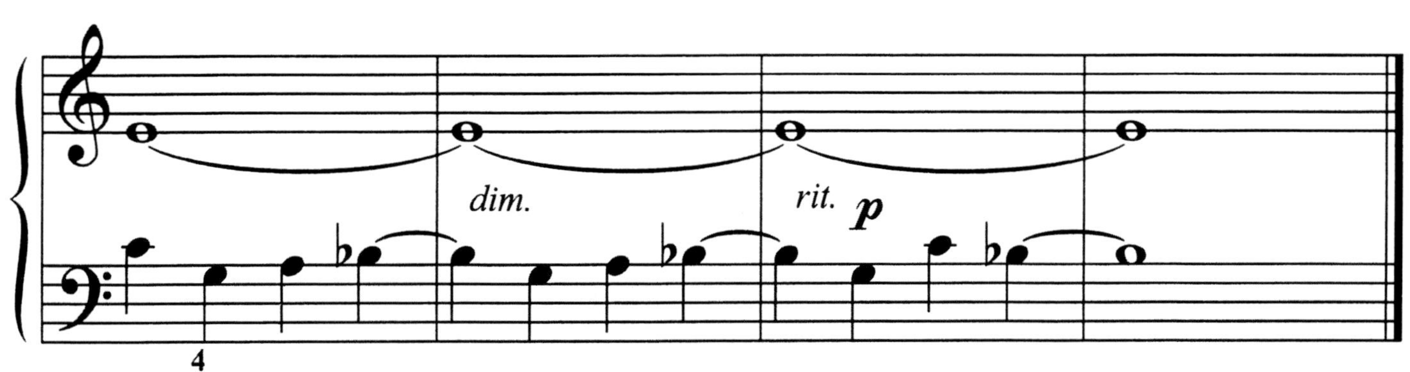
dim.
rit.
p

Jumping Bean

Giocoso

John Revezoulis

Feelin' Good Boogie

Spiritoso

John Revezoulis

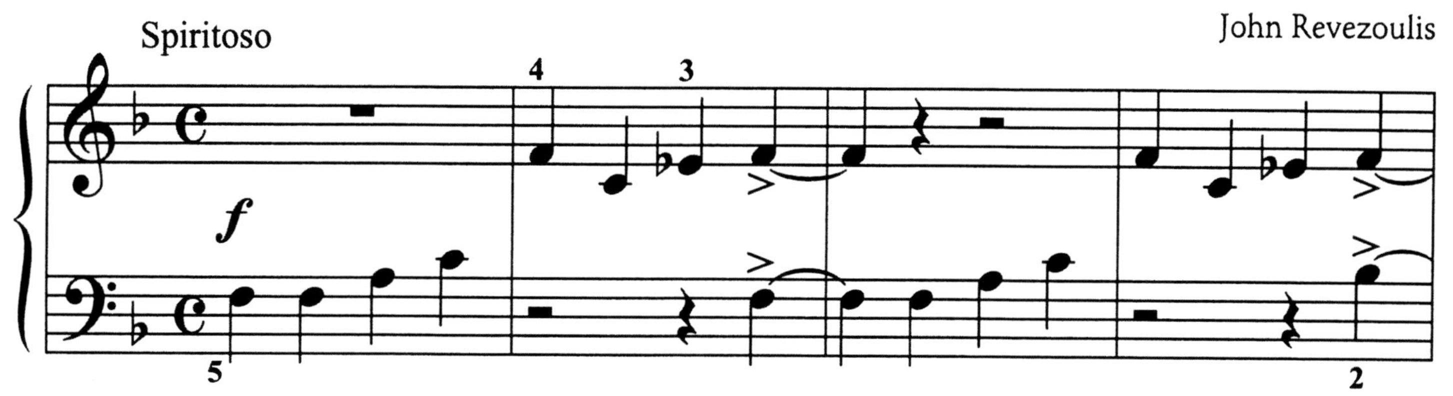

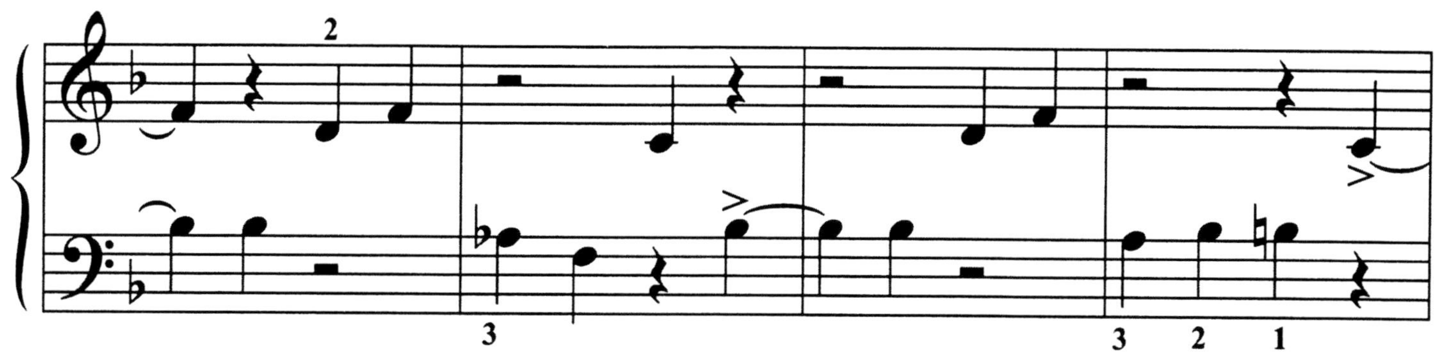

Lazy Blues

John Revezoulis

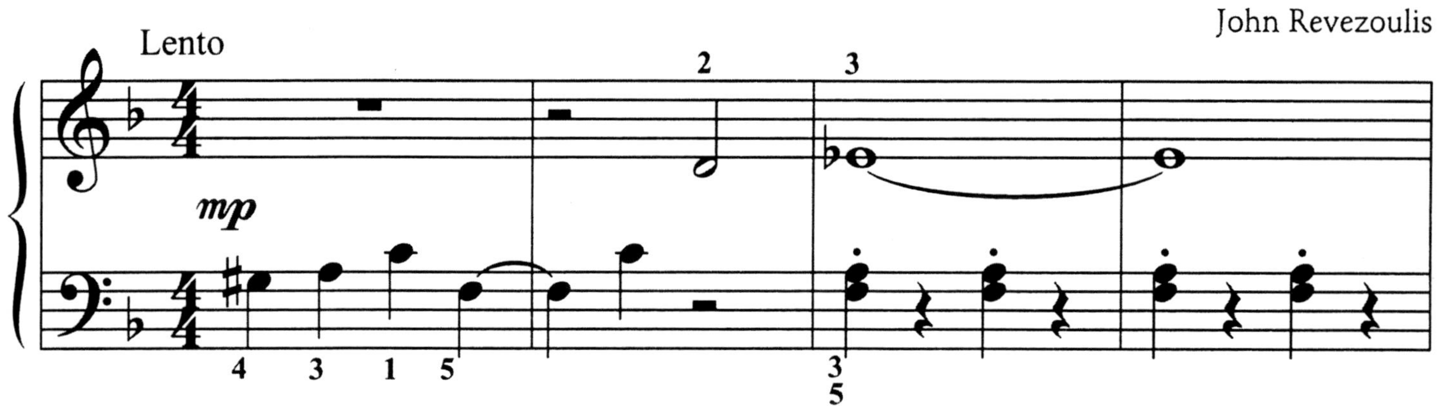

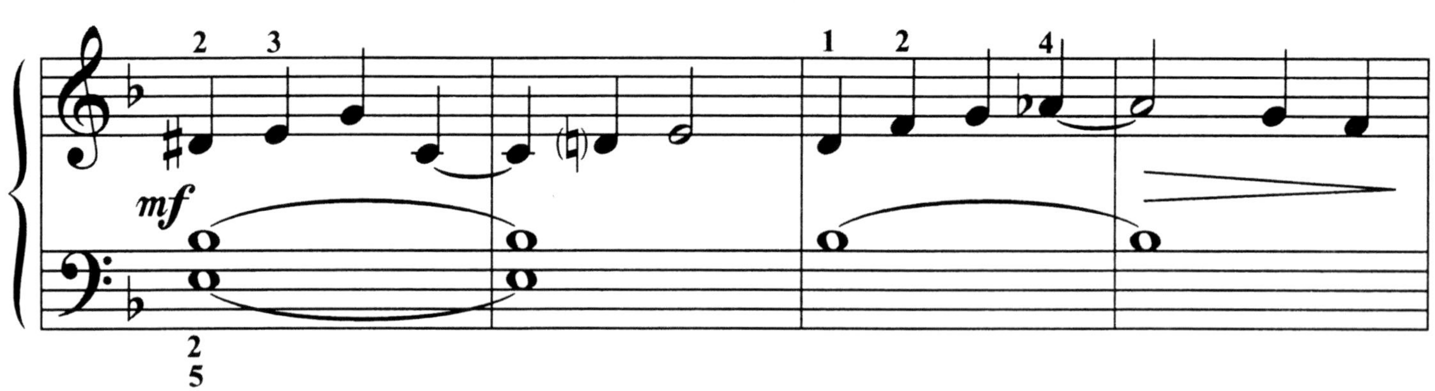

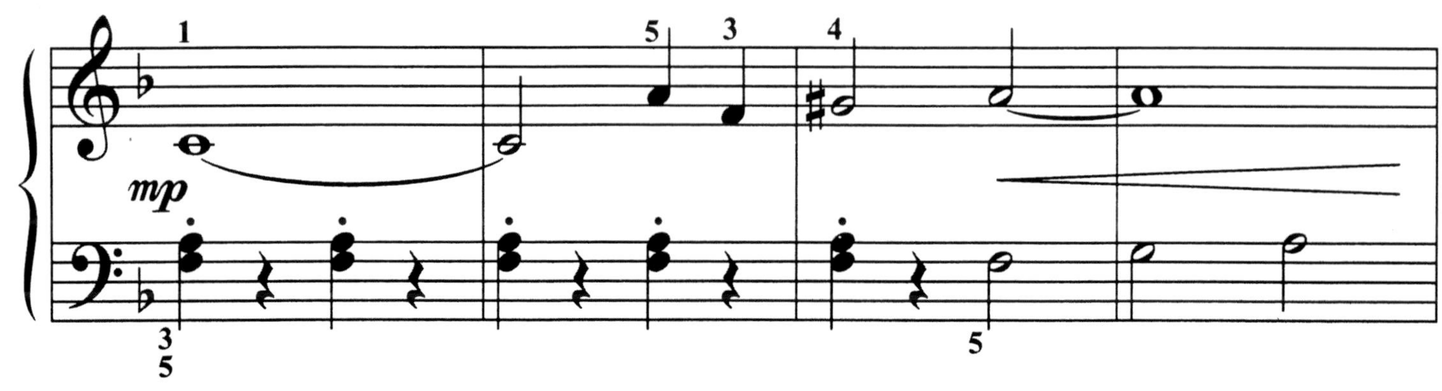

2
3
1
2
4
mf

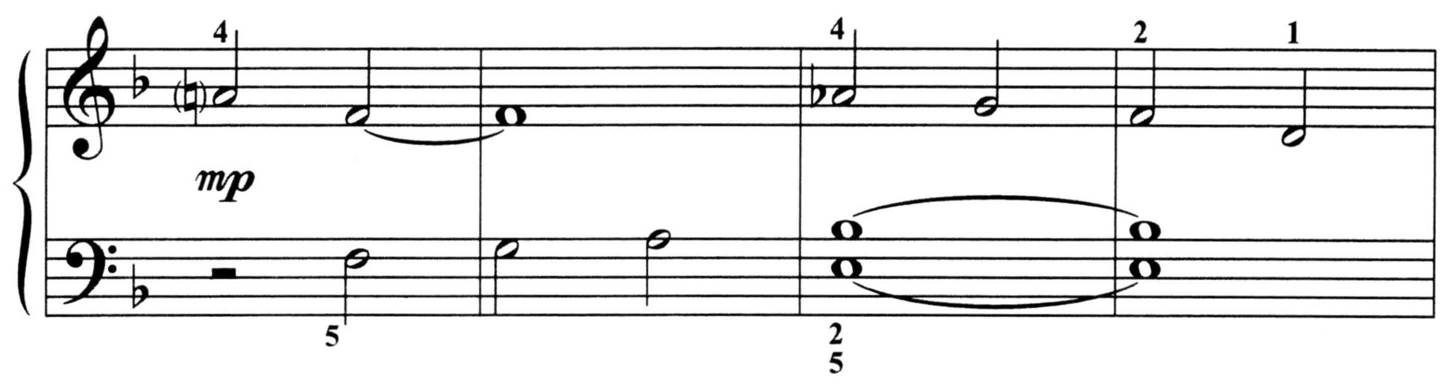
4
4
2
1
mp
5
2
5

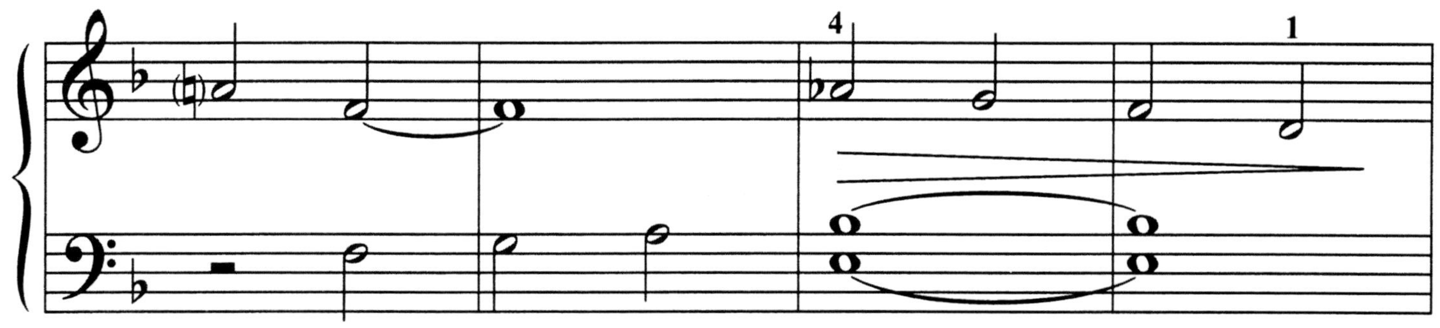
4
1

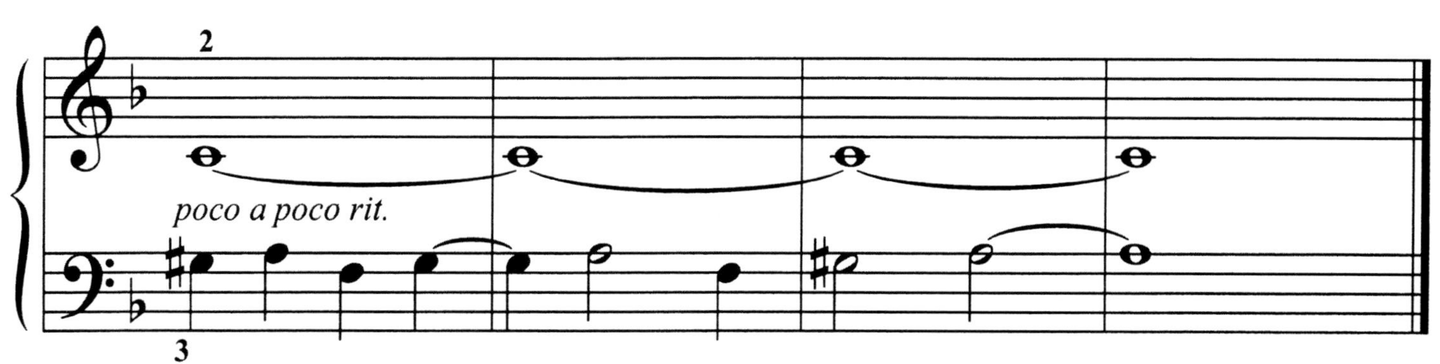
2
poco a poco rit.
3

Go For It

John Revezoulis

5
4
f
2
3
mp
f
poco a poco
cresc.
ff

Bossa Nova Rag

Andante

John Revezoulis

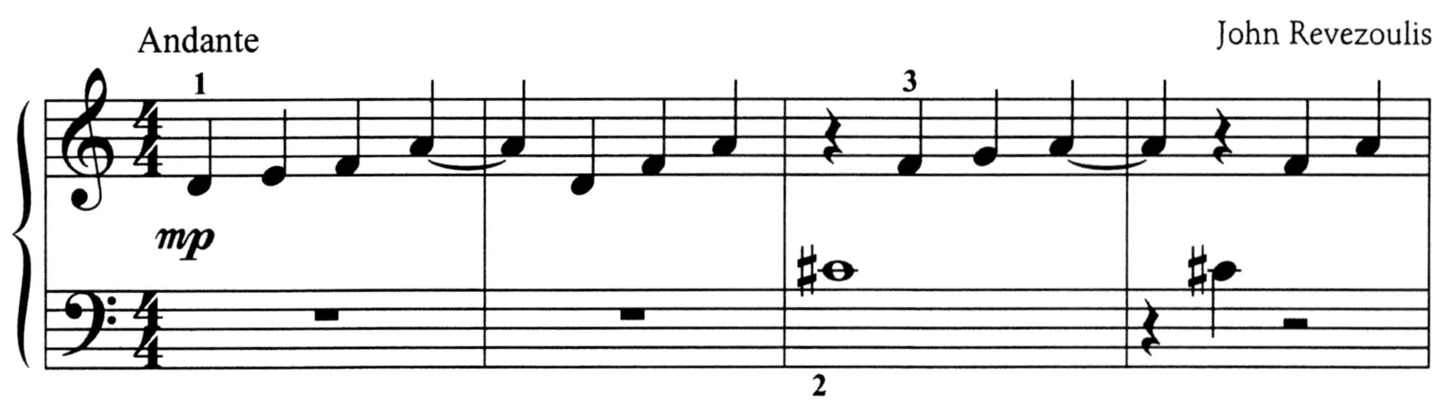

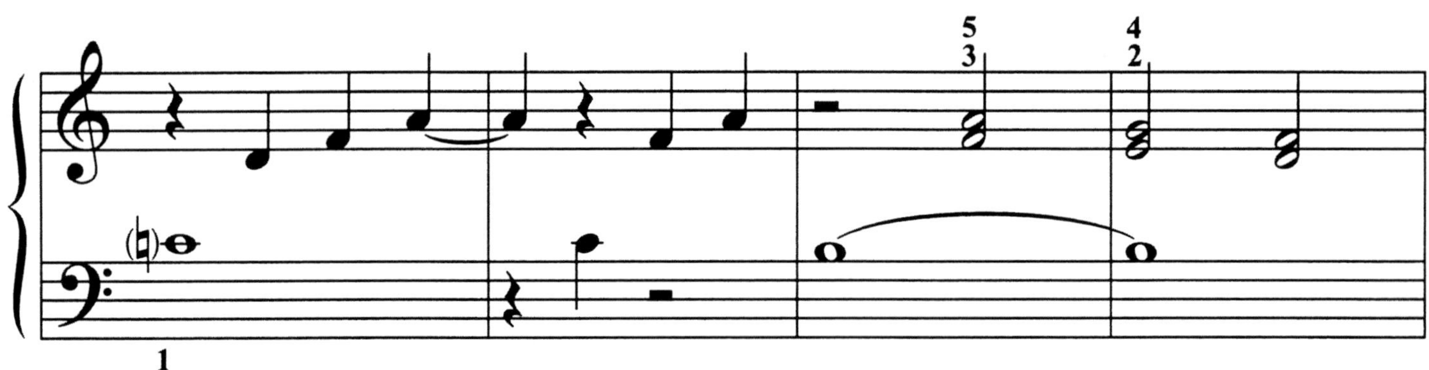

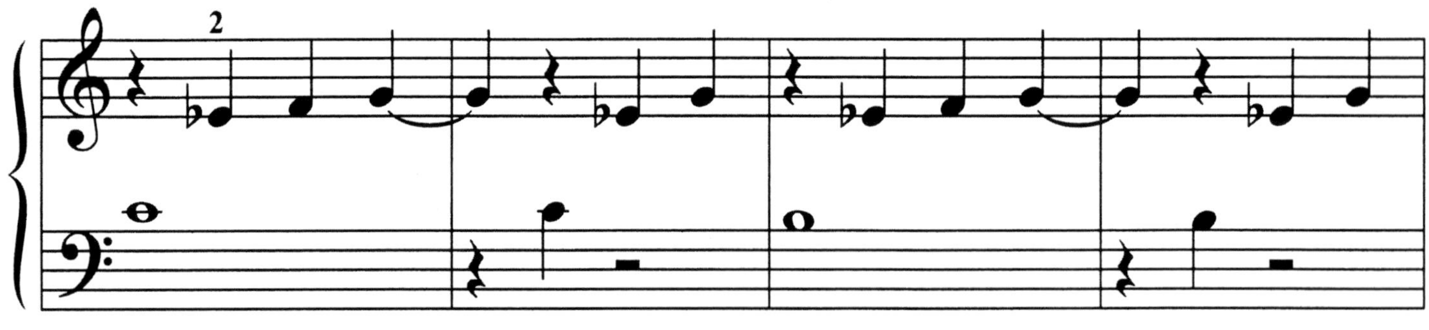

1
mf
2

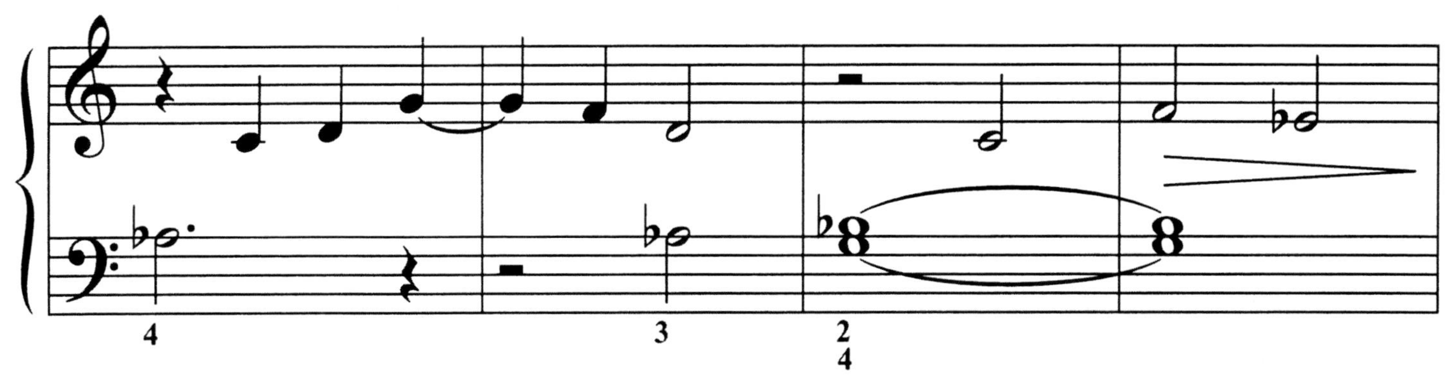
4
3
2
4

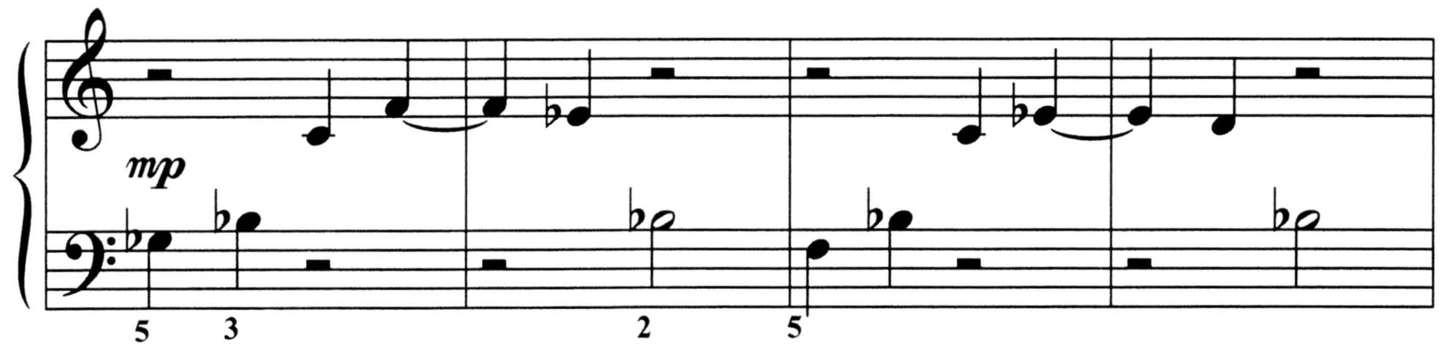
mp
5
3
2
5

1
5
3
5
2
4
1
rit.

Zig Zag Rag

Allegro

John Revezoulis

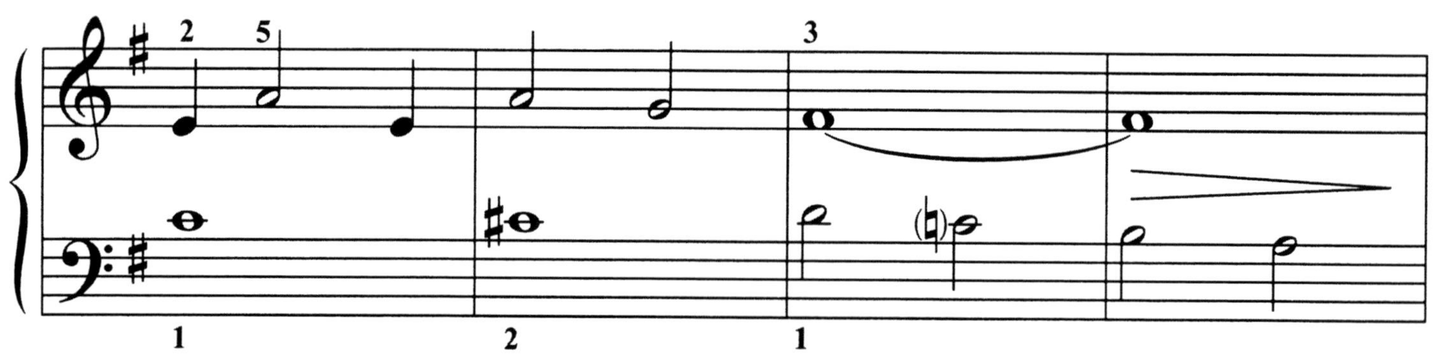

1
1
2
f
5
2

3
mf
2

4
p
poco a
poco crescendo
3
2

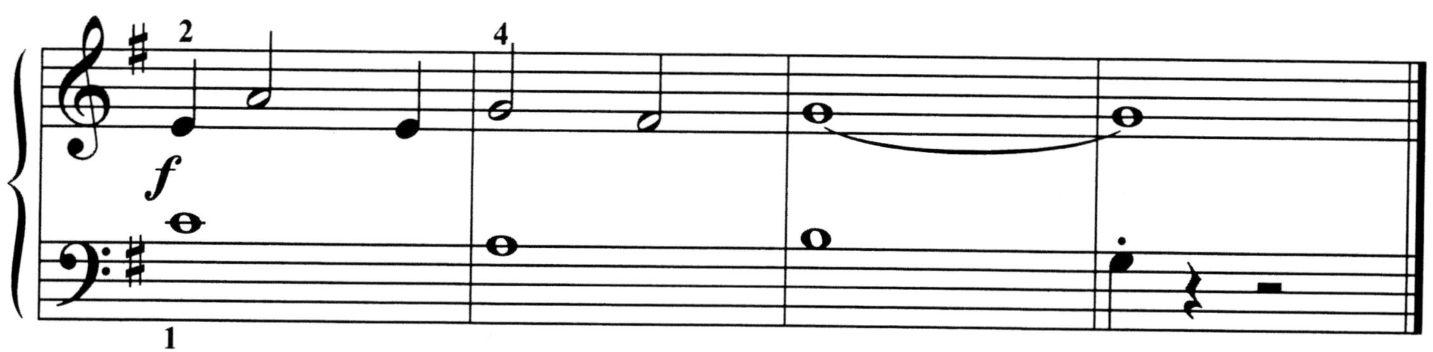
2
4
f
1

Bluesy Rock

Con Brio

John Revezoulis

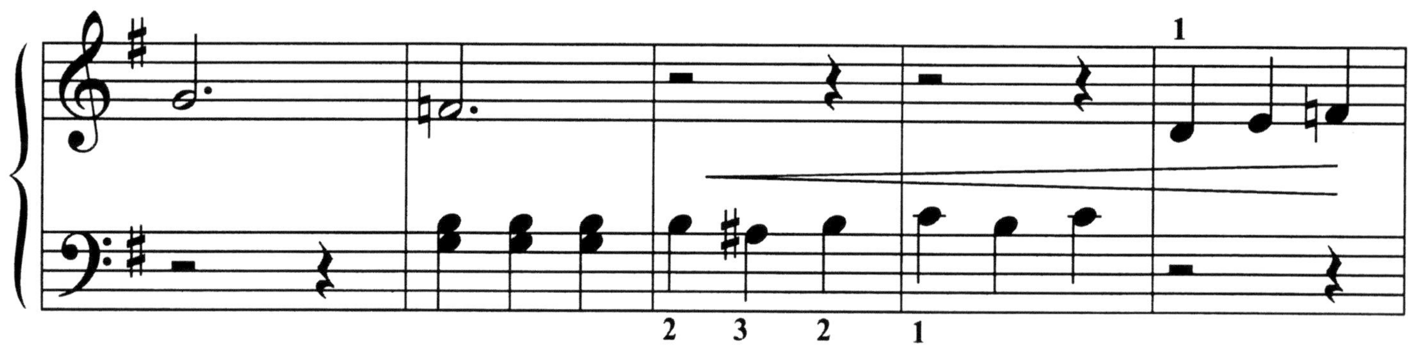

mf
2
4

1 2 3
2 3 2 1 2

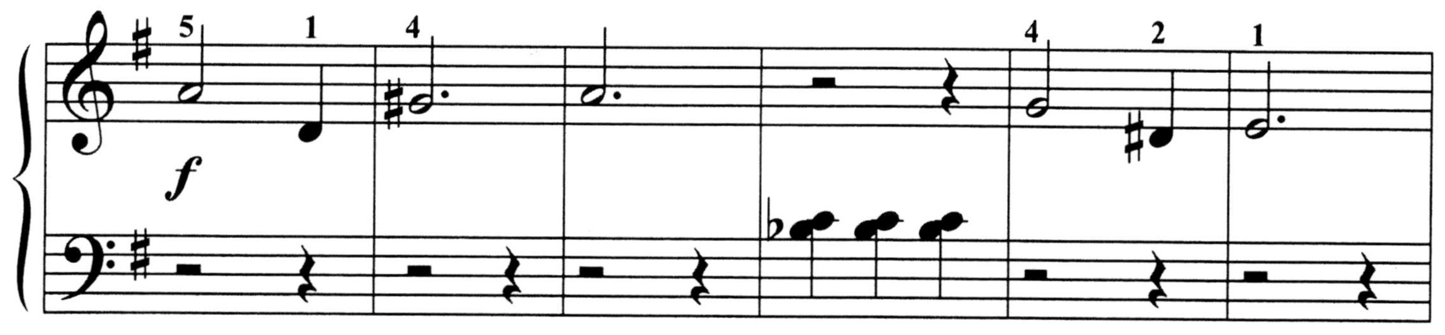
5 1 4
4 2 1
f

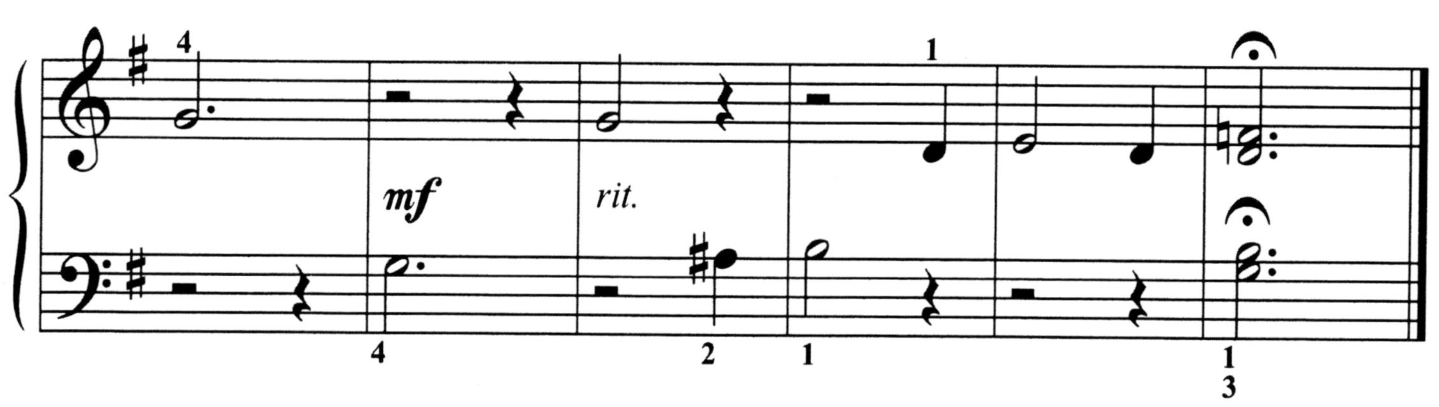
4
1
mf
rit.
4 2 1
1
3

Bare Bones Rag

John Revezoulis

Andante

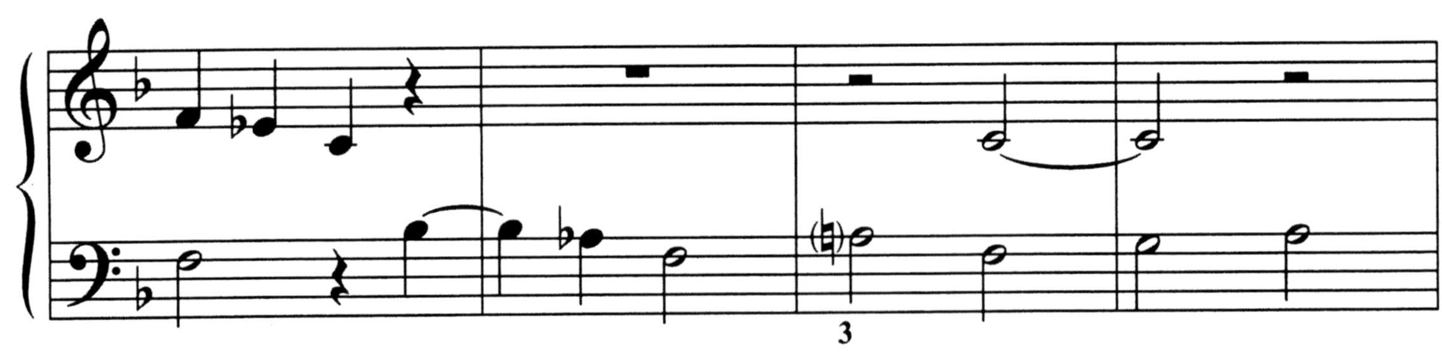

Wind Around

John Revezoulis

mp

poco a poco
crescendo

f

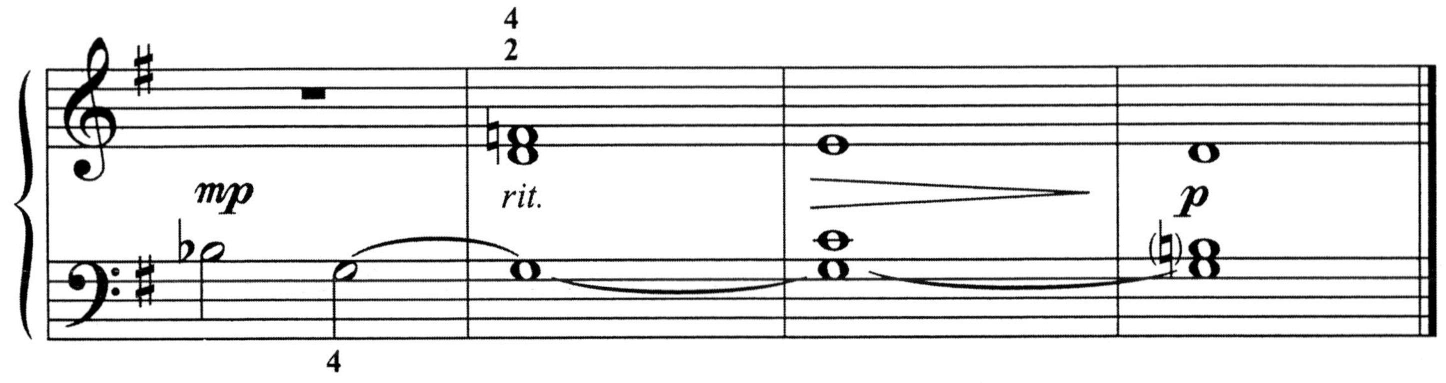
mp
rit.
p